JOYCE GRILL
RANDOM THOUGHTS

11 Original Piano Solos

D1003186

Random Thoughts is a collection of programmatic pieces that meet the technical and motivational needs of the intermediate student. These pieces offer refreshing and exciting repertoire that motivates students to excel, offers a variety a styles and keys, and presents music that is teacher tested. Here is innovative repertoire that keeps students practicing. The descriptive titles are designed to capture the imagination and nurture interpretive skills. The pieces should be played with a lot of flexibility as students try to show both mood and emotion. The pieces sound harder than they are and will give students a profound sense of accomplishment.

Rhythmic patterns including the dotted eighth followed by a sixteenth, swing eighths, combinations of triplets and duple eighths in the same measure, and rapid sixteenth-note groups are presented in 2/4 and 4/4 meters. Other concepts reinforced in this collection are overlapping pedal for chord changes, chromatic passages using harmonic thirds and sixths, chord inversions, arpeggios, dynamic playing across the range of the keyboard, and appropriate vocabulary usage for dynamic terms and tempo markings.

All of these pieces foster musical growth while providing students with an opportunity to use their imagination, focus on expression, and experience the joy of artistic performance.

Editor: GAIL LEW
Production Coordinator: KARL BORK
Art Design: CANDY WOOLLEY
Series Design: ROBERT RAMSAY

JOYCE GRILL

Joyce Grill is in high demand as a piano clinician, focusing on both teacher and student groups. As a former faculty member of the University of Wisconsin–La Crosse, Grill has had extensive hands-on teaching experience, which she brings to her clinics. As a result, she conveys not only course-related applications but also practical and tangible approaches to instruction and student development.

With degrees from the University of Wisconsin–Madison, Grill has had advanced study at the School of Fine Arts in Fontainebleau, France, where she studied with Nadia Boulanger (theory and composition) and with Robert and Jean Casadesus (piano). An active member of MTNA, Grill holds the MTNA Master Teacher Certificate.

Grill founded the LaCrosse Area Music Teachers Association. She also serves on the boards of the UW Music Alumni Association, the LaCrosse Public Education foundation, the WLSU Community Advisory Board, and the Viterbo College Bright Star Series. Grill is also a frequent guest conductor for multi-piano concerts and is active as a recitalist and accompanist for area faculty recitals and touring professionals.

Joyce Grill is a well-known composer whose various compositions for Warner Bros. Publications introduce students to the styles of several musical eras. Her original compositions, which are performed throughout the country, have been widely praised by both teachers and students. Her creative output includes a text on accompanying; solo and duet collections for the *WB Solo Library,* the *WB Duet Library,* and the *Composer Spotlight Series*; and many editions of original piano music written to address technical needs at different stages of musical development.

CONTENTS

GENTLE RAIN

JOYCE GRILL

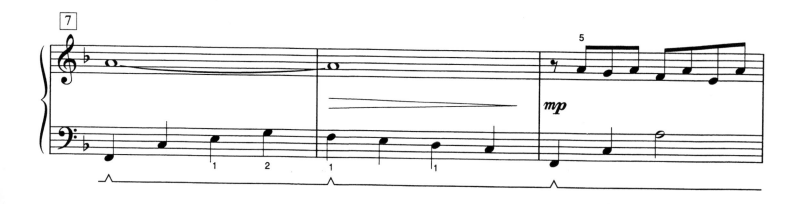

pedal simile

STROLLING ON THE AVENUE

JOYCE GRILL

I WISH I KNEW

JOYCE GRILL

GRAY SKIES

JOYCE GRILL

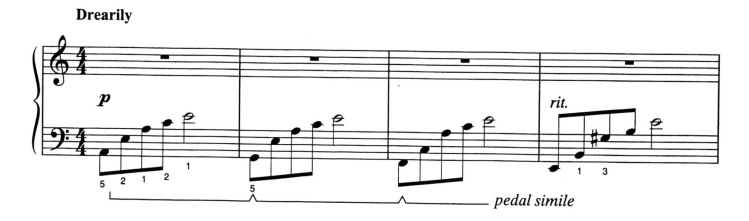

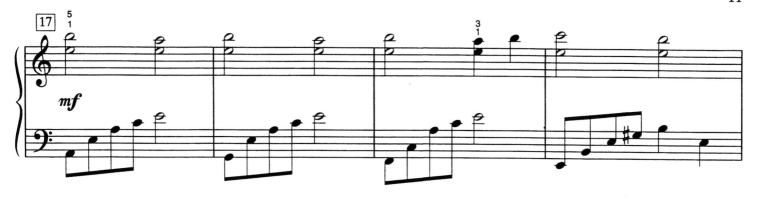

SOUTH OF THE BORDER

JOYCE GRILL

8va --------
senza pedale

THE GRAND BALLROOM

JOYCE GRILL

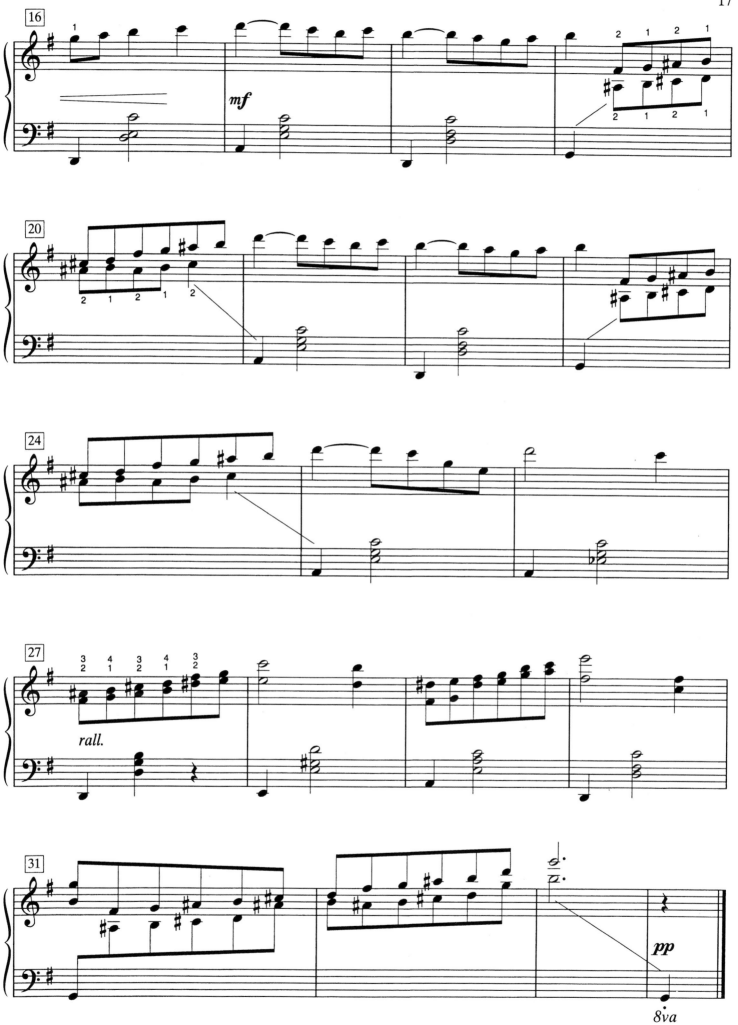

MELANCHOLY MINUTES

JOYCE GRILL

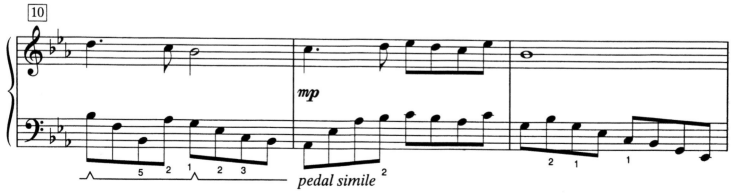

BITTERSWEET

JOYCE GRILL

ELM00007A

CLOSE TOGETHER

JOYCE GRILL

SHIMMERING WATERS

JOYCE GRILL

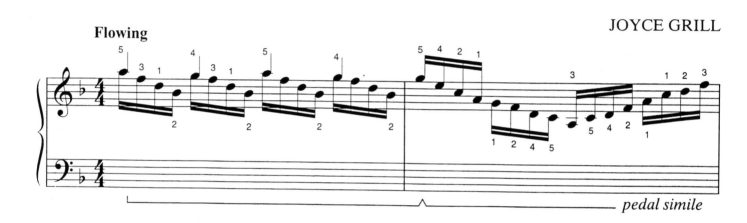

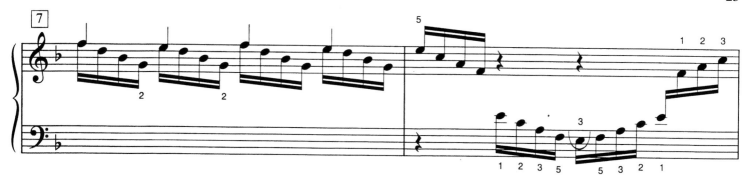

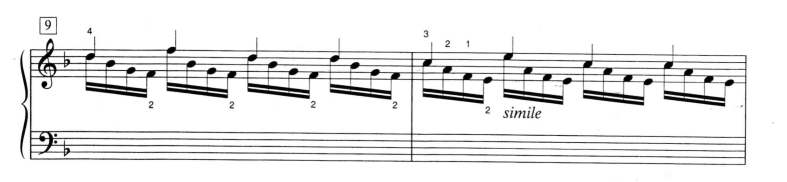

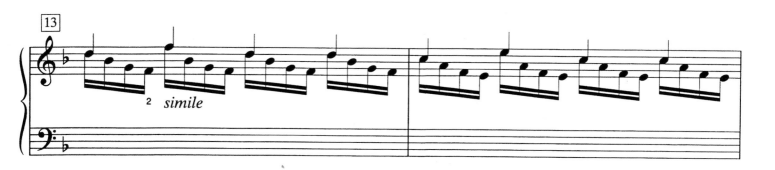

RANDOM THOUGHTS

JOYCE GRILL

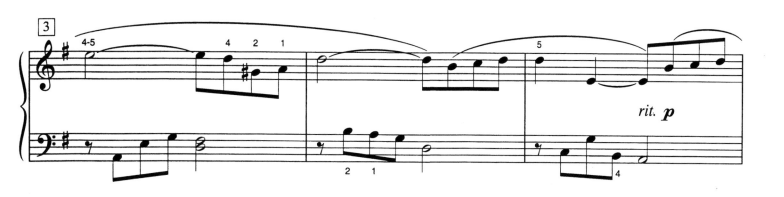

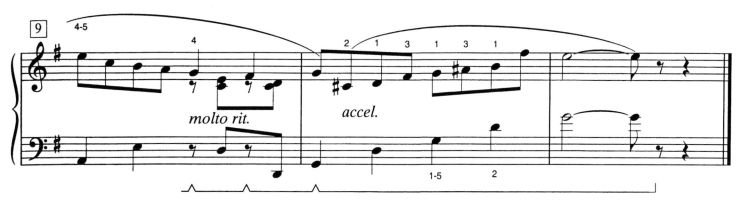

ELM00007A